WE'LL MEET AGAIN

Photographs of Daily Life in Britain During World War Two

IN THIS SERIES
*Published by Dent and drawn from the archives
of the Topham Picture Library*

The Day Before Yesterday 1850 to 1910   Introduced by Peter Quennell
Those were the Days 1914 to 1939   Introduced by Frances Donaldson
Memory Lane 1935 to 1953   Introduced by James Cameron
We'll Meet Again 1939 to 1946   Introduced by Robert Kee
Yesterday 1953 to 1970   Introduced by Benny Green

WE'LL MEET AGAIN

Photographs of Daily Life in Britain During World War Two

Introduced by ROBERT KEE

Picture Research and Captions by
Joanna Smith

J. M. Dent & Sons Ltd
London Melbourne

All the photographs are copyright and are printed from
negatives stored in the archives of the TOPHAM PICTURE
LIBRARY, P.O.B. 33, Edenbridge, Kent. They were taken
either by John Topham or the staff of Planet News with
the following exceptions:

Plate 19	Alfieri
Plates 48–9	Imperial War Museum
Plate 53	Associated Press
Plate 57	Imperial War Museum
Plate 58	London Transport Executive
Plate 59	Not known
Plate 60	Associated Press (Eddie Worth)
Plate 74	Sport & General
Plate 93	Imperial War Museum
Plate 94	Not known
Plate 95	Topical
Plate 105	Imperial War Museum
Plate 128	Imperial War Museum
Plate 144	Central News
Plate 182	Imperial War Museum
Plates 191–4	Pictorial Press
Plate 206	Imperial War Museum
Plate 207	U.S. Navy
Plate 214	Daily Mail
Plate 216	Associated Press
Plate 217	Manchester Public Library
Plate 218	BIPPA
Plate 234	Press Association

First published 1984
Introduction © Robert Kee 1984
Picture selection and captions © Topham Picture Library 1984

This book is set in 10/10½ Monophoto Apollo
Printed in Great Britain by
Jolly & Barber Ltd, Rugby, for
J. M. Dent & Sons Ltd
Aldine House, 33 Welbeck Street, London W1M 8LX

British Library Cataloguing in Publication Data

We'll meet again.
  1. World War, 1939–1945—Social aspects—
Great Britain—Pictorial works
941.084′022′2   DA587

ISBN 0–460–04649–7

Contents

Introduction by Robert Kee
'About the Photographs' by Joanna Smith

Introduction

The wonderful thing about these remarkable photographs is that, with only a few exceptions, they are not in any obvious way remarkable at all. What they do is simply to confer upon anyone lucky enough to turn the pages of the book a gift for the lack of which many an academic historian has failed his calling. They enable you to see history with the eye of someone who just happened to be passing at the time.

As the time was in fact the most momentous in the history of the British people it is a gift for which to be profoundly grateful. For anyone in their early forties or younger who feels as generations often do, haunted by their immediate past, and particularly that immediate past which was Britain's home front in the Second World War, here is an opportunity to reverse the process and haunt the past, to become a ghost or *revenant* in scenes which you never knew but feel you might have done.

Even when historic things are happening in the outside world human life is always a day-to-day affair, and it is that essential quality which is recaptured here. Look at the postman talking to the housewife outside her front door (plate 80). She is in curlers and smoking a cigarette like any housewife having a conversation with the postman – except that her front door isn't there any more. In its place there is just a mass of forlorn household wreckage, the work of a flying bomb which caused, as the newspapers put it, 'casualties and damage in southern England'. But it is the housewife and the postman that the photograph is about.

Or look at the expression on the face of the little girl (plate 138), as the Queen feels the texture of the dollar-earning frock which she is modelling for American export. It is not exactly clear what her thoughts are, except that they are the thoughts of a little girl not much concerned with dollars or her gracious Queen. On the other hand what the Royal Family truly meant to people in these years can be discerned in plate 76 – not so much from the good-natured expression of the King himself as from the faces of those talking to him in the devastation of their city.

History is about people and their experience of events, and the first condition for enjoying it is to acquire the feeling that the people to whom it is happening are alive like the people you know yourself. It is necessary to appreciate that the events were not experienced as history. For this, photography in the style of John Topham or the anonymous craftsmen of the Planet News Agency can be effortlessly helpful.

'Freeze-frame' is a device much used in motion picture editing to reveal paradoxically the fleeting quality of a moment by holding it. A camera in the hands of a competent stills photographer does this all the time. Even a quite humdrum picture can capture some of the myriad links in the infinite chain of moments of which human life and therefore history is composed. Take for instance plate 135 of Mr Duncan Sandys, the Minister of Works, talking to American troops clearing London rubble after the bombing. It is a small boy who steals the picture, being much more interested in the photographer than in either Mr Sandys, the GIs or even the woe-begone BBC engineer behind whom he is hiding. At the same time the boy wonderfully helps the photographer by emphasizing in contrast the un-camera-conscious faces of the GIs themselves as they pause in their dusty routine work to listen to their visitor. Further exploration discloses something about one of the young homburg-hatted Minister's legs, as the end of the stick he carries rests on the rubble beside him.

Such pictures quite often reveal a human touch of which the photographer at the time was probably unaware. In the picture of the naval Chief Petty Officer showing new recruits to the WRNS how to march (plate 96) the rawest ones still in their good sensible civilian clothes on the left are much more in awe of him than those in uniform further down the line who, momentarily out of sight, have heard it all before. Good photography often consists not only in the art which conceals art but in the art which conceals it even from the artist.

Thus if art is defined as seeing beyond the mere superficiality of the image, what primarily distinguishes a good photographer from a hack is awareness that in holding a camera he or she is in possession of a magic eye. Degrees of excellence will depend on awareness of situations in which that magic eye can work best. John Topham on a station platform from which young soldiers were going to the wars knew that with his picture of the vicar saying goodbye to his son (plate 21) he could capture much more than the fact of de-parture. In this book that magic eye is at the service of history.

Of course it tells us much more than simply that the people then were flesh and blood just as people are now. It can also dredge up bizarre curiosities such as the steel-helmeted and Wellington-booted 'Nazis' taken prisoner fighting in German streets (in Batter-sea) and the makeshift German fighter plane and its dummy airman downed in a London suburb when such sights were still in reach only of the imagination. And, still making the imagination boggle as once it did the censor's, there is the extraordinary sight of those coastal anti-aircraft gunners in drag (plates 158–9). Above all, though, for those who experienced this time in person, photographs revive the feelings that were in the mind when what was to become history was still the future.

The uncertainty, even fear, of the unknown with which the war began for Britain is now largely forgotten. Nothing very much was in fact to happen to Britain or British forces for many months after war was declared; history now calls the period 'the phoney war'. But few thought it would be like that when it started. The dire prognostications of statesmen and others throughout the earlier part of the year as to what was likely to happen should war come, were very similar to the sort of thing being said about the prospect of a Third World War today.

'When huge armaments are being piled up on every hand', Neville Chamberlain, the Prime Minister, had said, 'we cannot avoid a certain anxiety lest some incident, perhaps trifling in itself, should set in motion the machinery that would bring them into operation. We know that if that dread event should come to pass there would be none of those dearest to us who could count on escaping the consequences.' And the historian Arthur Bryant had written to *The Times* in April that a war 'with the destructive forces of modern science, would end in the destruction of European civilisation for all time'. Lord Elton wrote to *The Times* the next month to say that a world war 'must mean general anarchy, pestilence and famine for a generation'.

Enough had been heard and seen over the previous two-and-a-half years of the German and Italian bombing of civilian populations in the Spanish Civil War to lead people to expect devastation from the air. It was taken for granted that there might be gas as well as bombs. Gas masks were issued to civilians and armed forces alike. A million and a half gas helmets for children under two had been made – hoods fitted with a window to enclose the child's head, shoulders and arms – and a similar number of another model for children between two and four. Now that we know none of these were ever needed they just look faintly comic. But it was different at the time.

'This war', the Lord Privy Seal, Sir John Anderson, had said, 'will differ from anything this country has known for over a thousand years. It will be an invasion by air – sudden – swift and continuous. . . .' Nor was it only the appeasement-minded government and its supporters who conjured up such a spectre. The liberal *Manchester Guardian* had written in the summer: '. . . the fiercest bombing attacks on the great towns of this country – the lightning stroke intended to break us – will be made in the first days of war.' Twenty-one members of the medical staffs of London hospitals had written a letter to the press saying that no medical organization could cope with the probable number of casualties in air raids; some authorities estimated that there would be three psychiatric casualties for every physical one. As many as 200,000 casualties were expected in the first twenty-four hours.

These things were in the backs of the minds of the crowds (plate 6) waiting on 2 September 1939 outside Parliament where that evening Arthur Greenwood, 'speaking for England' as well as the Labour

Party, voiced deep disturbance that although Germany had attacked Poland thirty-eight hours before, thus automatically implementing our pledge to give Poland 'at once . . . all the support in our power', nothing had been done about it. And these sombre warnings must be remembered when you look at pictures of women filling sandbags, or washing up at territorial army camps or practising going to air raid shelters in those late summer days. No one who heard that first London air-raid warning twenty minutes after war was declared will ever forget it, or the strange bewilderment, relief and yet part-disappointment when nothing happened.

Nothing indeed happened for months, though the first air-raid casualty of a sort occurred before dawn the next morning when a policeman, seeing an un-blacked-out light on an upper floor of a house in Harley Street and getting no answer at the front door, tried to climb up the front of the building to put it out. He fell to the ground and was killed. But it was more than three months before the first British soldier was killed in action in France.

A sort of routine acceptance of the anti-climax quickly set in, engendering a mood which in a way was to serve the British people well for the rest of the war. For being able thus at their own pace to adjust a familiar way of life to the unfamiliar circumstances of war, with whatever twists and turns of fate it might yet bring, they were able to feel that the familiar British way of life was a good deal steadier and more secure than at times it really was – particularly during the summer of 1940.

On the home front the difficulties set in gradually; there was no rationing until January 1940. The fighting developed gradually too – if you could somehow forget about the unfortunate Poles, quickly buried with fine words of praise for their magnificent valour. First in April 1940 there was Norway. Chamberlain said that Hitler had 'missed the bus' there but it turned out otherwise, a bit of a cock-up for us instead. Such things were a familiar enough part of the British way of life. Then the French collapsed in June, but life went on: we played cricket at Eltham with the barrage balloon watching like a resting elephant; the Women's League of Health and Beauty put on their gas masks but did their stuff as usual.

I was being taught RAF drill on the front at Hastings at the time. You could hear the guns across the Channel at night. But we just marched and counter-marched, and on the day on which Churchill desperately tried to stop the French Government's rush for an armistice by offering France joint citizenship with Britain, our Flight Sergeant prefaced his traditional exhortative remarks with the words: 'Cheer up, lads! You're all going to be effing French men by midnight . . . kin'ell!' and we went on bashing up and down the front.

When the Battle of Britain vapour trails appeared in the skies behind St Paul's we watched and kept the score of German planes shot down as if it were a cricket match – unrealistically as we now know but the analogy kept morale high. At the airfield at which I was by then learning to fly, on the night in September in which there was a maximum invasion alert no one thought of giving us rifles with which to defend the place; we were simply sent to an air-raid shelter to await the dawn and another day much like the one before. It duly came. The invasion threat itself was real enough, and certainly our army was not in much of a state so soon after Dunkirk but somehow continuance of the British way of life seemed irrationally irrefutable. Dad's Army – seen here training to ward off German paratroopers with .22 miniature rifles – was a pretty faithful representation of the spirit of the time.

When the night raids on London intensified and at first met with little effective resistance, suddenly one night every anti-aircraft gun in the region opened up, whether it had a target or not, and we all felt much better watching the thousands of shells like little bright stars pricking the black sky, though they still weren't very effective. And, anyway, wasn't there that marvellous picture of St Paul's intact with the flames all round it? There were real air-raid casualties now (some 60,585 were killed in the whole war altogether but a single death was bad enough if you happened to see it yourself – like the poor woman with her feet sticking out from under the covering at Bexleyheath).

Through the stagnant years of 1941 and 1942 we soldiered on, doing well in the Middle East at times, less well at others, and not at all well most of the time against the Japanese. Yet, for all the set-backs, almost no one in these photographs at any time seriously doubted that we would win in the end. The Yanks came in – 'over-paid, over-sexed and over here'. Those who had been over here all the time, flying and fighting with the Eagle Squadron of the RAF, joined their own Air Force. Together we knocked Italy out of the war in September 1943 but the Germans somehow brought her back in again more than ever before. And all the time we wondered about and talked about and trained for and longed for the invasion of France. And then one marvellous day in June 1944 it

happened and before very long it began to look as if the end might really be in sight.

The failure at Arnhem and, a little later, the surprise German offensive in the Ardennes made us realize that it was not quite as much in sight as we had hoped. We acclimatized to the more distant prospect as we had acclimatized so long to the whole thing. We went on going to the rate-subsidized British Restaurants which were still serving cheap meals, although we no longer stole so many knives and forks from them as we had done in the days of the heavy air raids when so much cutlery needed replacing. We were beginning to look shabby. 'Shabbiness', wrote the *Manchester Guardian*, in January 1945, 'has descended deeply upon us . . . Scarcity of cosmetics and good stockings affects the appearance of our hard-working women . . .' Clothes rationing was as strict as it had ever been. If you used your coupons to buy a pair of stockings say every two-and-a-half months, you could buy a dress every nine months, some underclothing every four months and a night-dress every four years.

It was 'our great Russian allies' who broke the deadlock with the first of the Red Army's last two devastating offensives on 12 January 1945. Within weeks we and the Americans were across the Rhine, and on 8 May, shabby, weary but deliriously happy, we were at peace again in Europe – at peace in the whole world with the defeat of Japan in August.

Of course we had adjusted so well to the war over so long that it was going to be quite difficult now to adjust to the peace. We had 'met again', we had kept smiling through. But the position of Britain itself had changed greatly. *The Washington Post* had already written of the difficulty Britain was going to have realizing its weakened position as a military and financial power. 'She will emerge from the war a debtor nation, lacking the wherewithal to balance her external accounts without assistance. Moreover her export industries will be handicapped both by high labour costs and by technological backwardness.'

Maybe in peace it was not going to be quite so easy to keep smiling through after all. But at least, after nearly six years, the normality of war was over.

March 1984   Robert Kee

'About the Photographs'

Twelve thousand glass plate negatives, many still in envelopes unopened since they were stored away in the years of war, have been studied for the selection of photographs which appear in this book. The photographs, which are of considerable historical importance, are from two main sources. Many are the work of John Topham, a professional photographer working in the south of England and south-east London. His collection of some 500,000 negatives and prints, covering the period 1927 to 1970, is housed in the Topham Picture Library. In 1981 the Topham Picture Library added the million negatives which formed the archive of Planet News/UPI. These were photographed over the period 1930 to 1970, and it is from Planet News that the other photographs in this book have come. The two collections, one the work of an individual, the other the archive of a major international news agency, are complementary. An example of this is the difference in photographs taken to mark the outbreak of war. The Planet photographer recorded the anxious crowds in Parliament Square and the comings and goings of ministers and diplomats. John Topham noticed the parson saying farewell to his soldier son on Sidcup railway station (plate 21). Topham was deliberately seeking an image to sum up the impact of 3 September 1939 on ordinary people and to record it for history; in this he has brilliantly succeeded.

Very few of these photographs have been previously published. There are a number of reasons for this. Topham was working to record the importance of the events he witnessed, placed as he was on the front line of the battle for Britain. There was no market at the time for the bulk of his work. He had no staff to help him. He often had no time to caption and date his photographs. Even paper for photographic prints was in short supply.

Censorship was another factor, equally important to both Topham and Planet. It was frequently impossible for photographs to be published at the time and thereafter they were often forgotten. In the early years of war there was an understandable paranoia. Topham was arrested in Blackheath simply for having a camera. War artists were sometimes in fear of their lives as they attempted to record the Blitz. Even such an innocuous scene as an army officer receiving a report from an ambulance driver had to be submitted to the censor, and was returned by the censor with compliments before issue to the press 'passed'. Topham was not so lucky with plate 158. The idea of our gunners performing in drag presumably frightened the censor, if not Hitler. The Planet photographer's shot of the wing-commander who gallantly played the good fairy (plate 160) was so firmly censored that the negative remained in a sealed bag for forty years.

However, three pictures in *We'll Meet Again* are so outstanding that, although they have all been widely published, the book would be the poorer without them. Topham's picture of the children in the trench in the hop fields of Kent watching the Battle of Britain rage overhead (plate 54) had considerable impact in America. After the war this picture was used as a social document – showing the generation we were fighting for and for whom the future was to be built. The warden and child (plate 64) is a direct tug at the heart strings. The Planet News editor marked out all background material as can be seen in order to concentrate directly on the human drama. Plate 60 has been included because the sight of St Paul's towering above the inferno was to become the dominant image of the Blitz. Many similar photographs of this were taken. Some are doom-laden, full of menace, but this, with the great beacon of light and hope seeming to spring from the cross of St Paul's, is perhaps the most inspiring. A fourth picture (plate 211) is worthy of these three. Just as the separation on 3 September 1939 of father and son symbolized the beginning of the war so Bill's return seems to symbolize the end.

There have been difficulties in resurrecting these images of the war. The Planet collection suffered both bomb and flood damage and it is only recently that an effort has been made to halt the

deterioration which attacks the thin layer of gelatine carrying the image on the glass plate. Damp and heat are great enemies; mould flourishes, eating away the image (see above); as the gelatine expands and contracts a spider's web of reticulation appears on the picture (see over). In view of the historic importance of the pictures, those chosen have been printed warts and all so that there is no 'improvement' of history – the dust of time and the damage of war occasionally show.

Precise dating has frequently proved impossible; dates have often been deduced from internal evidence or from study of local press cuttings. Censorship has obliterated the location of many of the photographs so that we have often had to be content with 'somewhere in England'.

Our thanks are due to John Topham and the uncredited photographers of Planet News; to Lynne Burley, whose patience and skill in handling delicate negatives in a dark room for many months was exemplary. Born of a post-war generation, her excitement not

15

merely in seeing history come to life, but helping to rescue it from time, was infectious; to Alison and Michael Jones and my husband who worked hard to solve unnumbered mysteries; to Dent, our publishers, whose continual support has brought about what is now a growing photographic record of the past 130 years.

Our final debt is to Dame Vera Lynn who has allowed us to reproduce the World War Two portrait of herself and whose famous song 'We'll Meet Again' was frequently heard in our chilly negative room and dark room throughout the winter of 1983.

Joanna Smith

1. The Clouds of War

IN A BROADCAST FROM DOWNING STREET
AT 11.15 AM ON SUNDAY, 3 SEPT., 1939,
THE PRIME MINISTER SAID:-

'THIS morning the British Ambassador in Berlin handed the German Government a final Note stating that unless we heard from them by eleven o'clock that they were prepared at once to withdraw their troops from Poland a state of war would exist between us.

'I have to tell you now that no such undertaking has been received, and that consequently this country is at war with Germany.

'You can imagine what a bitter blow it is to me that all my long struggle to win peace has failed. Yet I cannot believe that there is anything more, or anything different that I could have done and that would have been more successful.

'Up to the very last it would have been quite possible to have arranged a peaceful and honourable settlement between Germany and Poland, but Hitler would not have it.

'He had evidently made up his mind to attack Poland whatever happened, and although he now says he put forward reasonable proposals which were rejected by the Poles, that is not a true statement.

'The proposals were never shown to the Poles, nor to us, and though they were announced in a German broadcast on Thursday night Hitler did not wait to hear comments on them, but ordered his troops to cross the Polish frontier. His action shows convincingly that there is no chance of expecting that this man will ever give up his practice of using force to gain his will. He can only be stopped by force.

'We and France are today, in fulfilment of our obligations, going to the aid of Poland, who is so bravely resisting this wicked and unprovoked attack on her people.

'We have a clear conscience. We have done all that any country could do to establish peace.

'The situation in which no word given by Germany's ruler could be trusted and no people or country could feel themselves safe has become intolerable.

'And now that we have resolved to finish it I know that you will all play your part with calmness and courage.

'At such a moment as this the assurances of support that we have recfived from the Empire are a source of profound encouragement to us.

'When I have finished speaking certain detailed announcements will be made on behalf of the Government. Give these your closest attention.

'The Government have made plans under which it will be possible to carry on the work of the nation in the days of stress and strain that may be ahead. But these plans need your help.

'You may be taking your part in the fighting services or as a volunteer in one of the branches of civil defence. If so, you will report for duty in accordance with the instructions you have received.

'You may be engaged in work essential to the prosecution of war, for the maintenance of the life of the people – in factories, in transport, in public utility concerns, or in the supply of other necessaries of life.

'If so, it is of vital importance that you should carry on with your jobs.

'Now may God bless you all. May He defend the right. It is the evil things that we shall be fighting against – brute force, bad faith, injustice, oppression and persecution – and against them I am certain that the right will prevail.'

1. Tableau of war veterans, VADS, ARP wardens, Britannia and civic dignitaries at the Regal cinema, Bexleyheath, April 1939. The same month Neville Chamberlain announced, in the House of Commons, limited conscription in response to the German threat to Poland.

Labour and Liberal members opposed the measure but over 300,000 young men were called up.

2. Holiday crowds at Southend-on-Sea cheered the town's hospital carnival procession in the August heat. War was declared eleven days later. 'I do not recall any period when the weather was so hot', wrote Churchill. 'It was indeed just the weather that Hitler wanted for his invasion of Poland.'

3. In expectation of massive air raids householders busily fill sandbags by the light of a paraffin lamp. The hole could be used for an air-raid shelter.

4. The casualty room of the
Livingstone Hospital, Dartford,
Kent, protected by sandbags,
29 August, 1939.

5. 30 August: soldiers on guard at
a London railway station used a
waiting room for stores and
equipment.

6. Saturday, 2 September, 1939. Both Houses of Parliament met to pass the Bill empowering the Government to conscript all men between the ages of 18 and 41, as anxious crowds waited in Parliament Square.

7. Meanwhile the Guards at Buckingham Palace wore steel helmets for the ceremony of the Changing of the Guard, 2 September, 1939.

8. Would-be Army recruits at the Central Recruiting Depot in Scotland Yard were told to wait for their call-up notices.

9. Territorial recruits joining up in Sidcup.

10. Anti-Aircraft display and filmshow at the State cinema, Dartford.

11. Boys played at war wearing tin hats, which could be bought at toyshops, September 1939.

12. Territorials at a training camp near Chichester in August had a gas mask inspection.

13. Foot inspection of Royal West Kent Territorials at the summer camp of 1939 at Lympne.

14. Women volunteers washing up at the Chichester Territorial camp.

15. Territorials' motor cycle inspection at Lympne.

16. Air raid practice: a master takes the roll call. More air-raid shelters for the 960 boys and girls of the school were being constructed but at the beginning of this autumn term of 1939 there was only room for 120 children in the shelter so sixty girls and sixty boys were allowed into school at any one time and school was run on a shift system.

17. Evacuation of London children, September 1939. Almost 1,500,000 people, mostly children, were evacuated from the cities, most of them between 1 and 3 September, under the Government scheme.

18. Evacuees at Wye. The children
are from Catford.

19. Some children were sent abroad, many to Canada.

20. Greenwich Hospital nurses off to country quarters by double-decker bus.

2. Braced for Action

THE whole fury and might of the enemy must very soon be turned on us. Hitler knows that he will have to break us in this island or lose the war. If we can stand up to him, all Europe may be free and the life of the world may move forward into broad, sunlit uplands. But if we fail, then the whole world, including the United States, including all that we have known and cared for, will sink into the abyss of a new Dark Age made more sinister, and perhaps more protracted, by the lights of perverted science. Let us therefore brace ourselves to our duties, and so bear ourselves that, if the British Empire and its Commonwealth last for a thousand years, men will still say, 'This was their finest hour.'

WINSTON CHURCHILL.
From a speech in the House of Commons, 18 June, 1940.

21. A Territorial leaving to join his regiment. John Topham, the photographer, wrote, 'This picture was taken at Sidcup station on the day that war broke out – 3 September 1939 and shows the local parson saying his farewells to his son – a Territorial in the Artists' Rifles.' Topham's aim that day, as for all photographers, was to produce a commemorative picture.

22. Local Defence Volunteers practise rifle shooting, 24 June 1940. The LDV force, for which Churchill had been pressing since October 1939, was formed immediately he became leader. Anthony Eden broadcast an appeal for volunteers on 14 May 1940; within twenty-four hours 250,000 men had enlisted. On Churchill's insistence, the force was renamed the Home Guard and this was the official name from 23 July 1940.

23. Preparing for the Luftwaffe: anti-aircraft gun emplacement near London.

24. Gunners await low-flying aircraft over the Thames.

25. Scots Guards training in August 1941 before joining their service battalions.

26. Paratroopers training at a military training school in the north-west. Suspended on steel cables, the trainees' rate of descent is controlled by airbrake to give the impression of falling at the same rate as the actual jump from an aircraft.

27. ARP exercise in a London suburb: a model of a German aeroplane and its Swastika-d 'crew', April 1940.

28. A realistic ARP exercise in London's Old Kent Road, organized by Camberwell Council in October 1939 – helping burn 'casualties'.

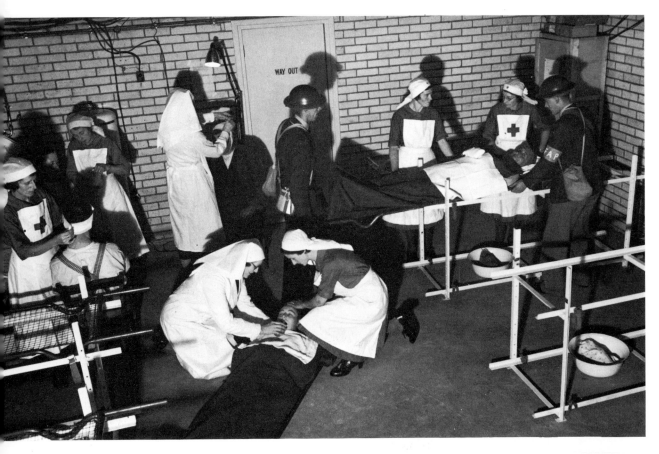

29. 'Victims' at an emergency underground hospital at Erith: the receiving room with stretcher-bearers depositing their burden on one of the specially constructed stands, October 1939.

30. The Auxiliary Fire Service at Church End, Finchley, converted a second-hand car and a collection of old junk into a fire engine for a total cost of £2.10.0d. (£2.50). It was first in service in December 1940.

31. Boat drill on dry land for recruits to the Royal Marines at a port in southern England, March 1940. 'The all-rounders of Britain's forces', said the contemporary caption.

32. As Britain awaited invasion in 1940, attempts were made to deny the German airforce landing grounds. Among other measures, wires were stretched across roads which might be used as runways.

33. Barrage balloons were flown up to a height of 12,000 feet to force enemy aircraft to fly high over target areas and avert precision in their bombing raids. This was a mobile balloon with its crew.

34. Sandbagged air-raid shelter in a disused railway tunnel in Kent which used to lead to chalk pits.

35. As women worked in the war effort, day nurseries were provided for their children. Teachers and schoolgirls gave up their summer holiday in 1940 to look after Dartford children in this day nursery, collecting the children at 8 am and taking them home at night. The dug out air-raid shelter was nicknamed the 'Goblins' House' and air-raid practice was disguised as a game.

36. Mother and child outside their garden air-raid shelter, the 'Ritz Hotel', Downham.

37. An Auxiliary Fire Service post in a private semi-detached house used an old taxi as its fire engine.

38. First aid post in a Sidcup home, 'The Strand Palace'.

39. Women ambulance drivers in Gravesend listen to a briefing from their officer.

40. Old cars parked across a level field in southern England to prevent German aircraft from landing.

41. Women of the Auxiliary
Territorial Service at gas mask
drill. The ATS, originally
volunteers, were admitted to full
military status in 1941, renamed
the Women's Royal Army Corps
after the war in 1949, and have
been an integral part of the British
Regular Army ever since.

42. Travellers to London by train
lost 500 gas masks in one month
alone; a baby's mask was among
those photographed at a railway
lost property office, January 1941.

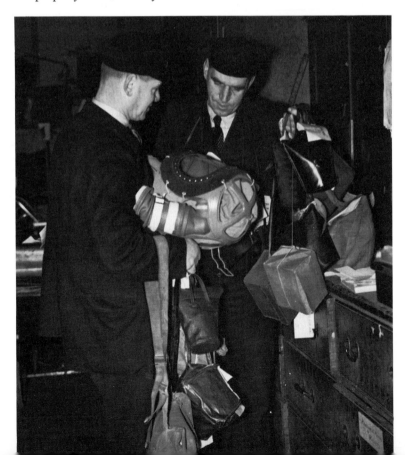

43. First prize at a National Service
display went to a miniature AFS
fire engine.

44. Camouflaged public house:
The Northover at Downham.

45. Tent into haystack – an
ingenious method of camouflaging
an anti-aircraft encampment.

46. London Transport parked its buses in the streets, to reduce the risk of losing large numbers of vehicles through a direct hit on a garage. The poster on the front of the bus was one of the most famous wartime slogans.

47. Wardens great and small. Miss Allnutt, 6′2″ tall, towered over her male colleague and was thought to be the tallest female warden in the country.

48. Anti-gas ointment for emergency use against mustard gas splashes on the skin: the ointment had to be rubbed into the skin within five minutes.

OINTMENT ANTI-GAS Nº 2
APPLY FREELY TO AFFECTED
PORTION OF SKIN
AS SOON AS POSSIBLE
RUB IN UNTIL OINTMENT IS ABSORBED
AVOID CONTACT WITH EYES

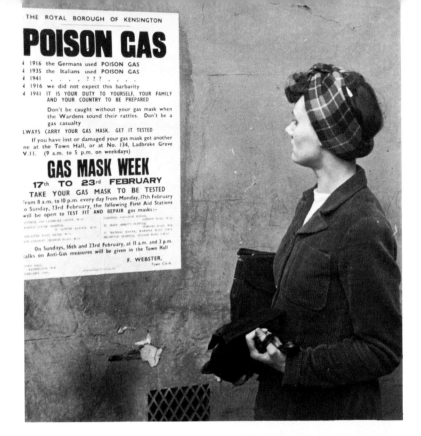

49. 1941 poster warning the public of the danger of poison gas attack.

50. 1939 police poster with details of blackout regulations for buildings and vehicles. An Ealing man was sentenced to one month's hard labour in February 1940, for allowing light to be seen from his home, while road accidents increased sharply. Six deaths were reported, in the first months, of pedestrians colliding with solid objects.

3. Under Attack

10, DOWNING STREET,
WHITEHALL.

ON what may be the eve of an attempted invasion or battle for our native land, the Prime Minister desires to impress upon all persons holding responsible positions in the Government, in the Fighting Services, or in the Civil Departments, their duty to maintain a spirit of alert and confident energy. While every precaution must be taken that time and means afford, there are no grounds for supposing that more German troops can be landed in this country, either from the air or across the sea, than can be destroyed or captured by the strong forces at present under arms. The Royal Air Force is in excellent order and at the highest strength it has yet attained. The German Navy was never so weak, nor the British Army at home so strong as now. The Prime Minister expects all His Majesty's servants in high places to set an example of steadiness and resolution. They should check and rebuke expressions of loose and ill-digested opinion in their circles, or by their subordinates. They should not hesitate to report, or if necessary remove, any officers or officials who are found to be consciously exercising a disturbing or depressing influence, and whose talk is calculated to spread alarm and despondency. Thus alone will they be worthy of the fighting men, who in the air, on the sea, and on land, have already met the enemy without any sense of being out-matched in martial qualities.

July 1940.   WINSTON CHURCHILL

51. Anti-aircraft gunners
celebrating their success in
bringing down three Dornier 17
bombers, September 1940. The
men, former Territorials, were for
the most part no more than
nineteen or twenty years old, and
they had been on duty all night
on their gun site near Rochester
before the Dorniers appeared.

52. 'Still in Good Heart' was the
verdict of the caption writer on
this picture of men back from the
hell of the Dunkirk beaches June
1940.

53. Scots gather round a German
reconnaissance plane which was
shot down by the RAF after a
running fight, 18 October, 1939.
The pilot survived and was taken
prisoner.

54. Children sheltering in a trench dug in the hopfields of Kent, watch the air battle as Spitfires intercept enemy bombers, September 1940. This is one of the famous images of the war. It was published by *Life* Magazine on 23 September, 1940 under the headline 'Hitler Tries To Destroy London' and was used as a propaganda poster by Americans involved in the campaign to 'Defend America by Aiding the Allies'. The slogan was: 'Help England – and it won't happen here.' The photographer was John Topham.

55. A family of five, plus dog, in their air-raid shelter which measured 7 feet by 5 feet. They had electric light, a radio and a bottle of beer.

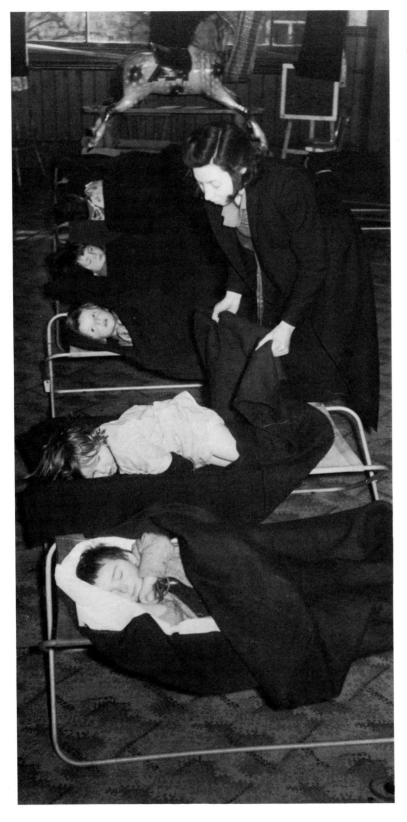

56. At St Nicholas Nursery Centre, Guildford, in February 1941 the children of evacuated mothers were accommodated in rooms hastily set up to receive them as part of a campaign by the Nursery Schools Association to enable mothers to continue with war work. Still in their day clothes, the children are being put to sleep on camp beds wrapped in blankets – bedding barely adequate for a February night.

57. Elephant and Castle Underground Station during the Blitz, 11 November 1940. 4,588 people died from air bombardment in Britain in this month alone.

58. Tube refreshment depot which provided food and drink, night and morning, for workers and those who used the tube for shelter.

59. The dome of St Paul's against a scrawl of vapour trails.

60. Symbol of resistance; St Paul's Cathedral ringed by the fires of the Blitz, 7 June 1941, with the clouds of smoke miraculously parted. Photographed by Eddie Worth, this is another of the famous images of the war.

61. St Bride's Church, off Fleet Street, February 1941. A policeman acts as guide to the Australian journalist Colin Wills and Robert McCall (left), manager of the Australian Broadcasting Commission of Victoria.

62. The destruction of a church in Kent.

63. Sidcup blacksmith Doug
Holland carries on amid the
bombed ruins of his forge.

64. A woman rescue worker holds a terrified child, perhaps the most intense image of the home front war, after a V1 attack, Buckingham Gate, Victoria, 23 June 1944.

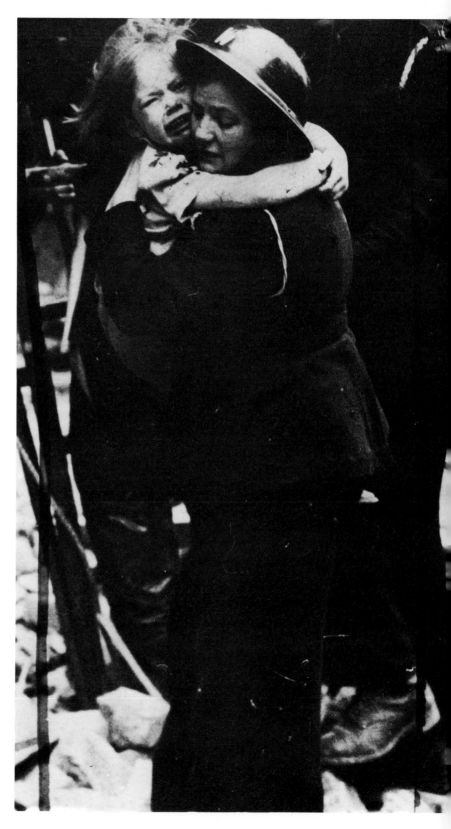

65. Corpse of a woman killed in a Bexleyheath bombing.

66. Rescue workers bringing a survivor out of the ruins of a factory in Bexleyheath 1940.

67. A woman is lifted from the
factory rubble onto a stretcher.

68. A home-made bomb shelter
intact among the ruins,
Bexleyheath.

69. Wendell Wilkie, Roosevelt's recent opponent for the American Presidency, arrived in England in January 1941 with a friendly letter from the President for Churchill. He is seen here walking through the ruins of Coventry Cathedral with the Bishop of Coventry. Churchill spoke of Wilkie's visit and the mission of the President's envoy, Harry Hopkins, in a broadcast of 9 February. 'We may be sure that they will both tell the truth about what they have seen over here, and more than that we do not ask.'

70. A pile of bomb rubble by the Thames at Lambeth seems almost to dwarf the Palace of Westminster.

71. Fleet Street closed for bomb clearance, 15 October, 1940.

72. Leicester Square on the
morning of 17 April 1941.
450 German war planes took part
in one of London's worst air raids
of the war on the previous night.
It was one of a succession of raids;
Coventry and Bristol were bombed
on 8 and 11 April, the Belfast
dockyards on 15 April and
Portsmouth on 17 and 27 April.
Civilian deaths in Britain from
bombing in April 1941 totalled
6,065.

73. Firemen at work in Holborn
after the raid of 16 April, 1941.

74. Attacking warehouse fires
from boats on the Thames.

75. Dover under fire. The town was within reach of German guns from occupied France, as it was discovered in August 1940 when the Germans first attempted to close the Straits of Dover to Allied shipping. The inhabitants of the town soon became used to the sign 'Shelling in progress, take cover', and through binoculars, on fine days, German tanks, mines and troops could be seen from the white cliffs in which many of the population sheltered from bombs and shells.

76. King George VI visiting
bombed areas of Bristol which on
the night of 11 April 1941 suffered
'devastation such as I had never
thought possible' (diary of Sir John
Colville, 12 April, 1941).

77. Churchill goes out to see for
himself after a bombing raid.

78. January 1941: a London woman posed for the photographer after a daylight attack with incendiary bombs had been tackled by housewives who managed to extinguish the fires with stirrup pumps and sand.

79. Mr and Mrs Crist and their three sons were asleep in their Anderson shelter in Bromley when a bomb fell just beside them on 15 October 1940; they all escaped without a scratch.

80. By the middle of May 1941 the worst of the London Blitz was over; the 'little Blitz' of January – April 1943 was distressing while it lasted but it faded away with the increasing weakness of the Luftwaffe. Yet the arrival of the first of the V1 flying bombs, or 'buzz bombs' as they were called, in the early hours of Tuesday, 13 June 1944 heralded for Londoners some of the most terrifying and destructive times of the war. This was the scene outside a block of flats which had received a direct hit, causing deaths and damage. Amidst the pathetic debris were prams, a child's high chair and a doll's cot. The postman makes enquiries.

81. Bomb damage repair on the railway. A priority was to keep the essential services – water, gas, electricity and transport – going in spite of the air-raids.

82. Captured German airmen on their way to an internment camp, 8 February 1941. The cardboard boxes contained their personal possessions.

83. Machine gun ammunition
arriving to re-arm a Blenheim
bomber, 16 August, 1941. The
British bombers were armed with
machine guns which could, at the
cost of some loss of speed, enable
them to retaliate against enemy
fighters.

84. A briefing session for bomber
crews, 16 August, 1941.

85. The weary faces of pilots listening to a briefing.

86. Fighter pilots disperse.

87. Some of the 'Few';
602 Squadron.

4. Shoulder to Shoulder

Now, let us take stock of ourselves. We have our backs to the wall surely enough. You know that, all of you – men and women. You know what is at stake. You know what fate awaits us if those ruthless desperadoes succeed in making us the next victims of their juggernaut ride to world mastery and the enslavement of all mankind. If they could, they would yoke us in bondage to their war machine, setting us to turn out bombs to drop on our friends elsewhere, as other people are being slave-driven to make arms for use against us. You know, too, that we are fighting against odds at this moment. Many of you have fought and planned and toiled for some years to make us ready. Our heavy industry has been replanned. Stocks of raw materials have been built up. Thousands of men have worked long intense hours on the benches and machines at the Royal Ordnance and other factories. I am fully mindful of their devoted effort. But the enemy had a long start in the race to prepare for this war, and we have not yet caught him up. You read and hear, day by day, how our magnificent young men are striving to buy with their flesh and blood the time that we need to build up our strength. At this hour of all hours, we at home cannot take things easy, for whether we have deserved it or not, the men of our fighting forces are struggling to give us time to make up leeway, to their undying honour. What are we doing to go with it – with this crucial time that we yet possess? The question answers itself. We, men and women alike, are going to work our fingers to the bone for our sons and for their future. We are going to do whatever lies in our power to match, and to be worthy of, the sacrifices that are being made for us. We are going to cut down our leisure, cut down our comfort, blot out of our thought every private and sectional aim. We must. We are going to guard our health and strength: for these are assets in the fight. But we shall be careless of all else – thinking only of arms for the men, arms for victory, arms for liberty. After all, these young fighting men are our sons. We bred them; there must be something of their spirit in us. ...

HERBERT MORRISON'S *radio broadcast*,
22 May 1940.

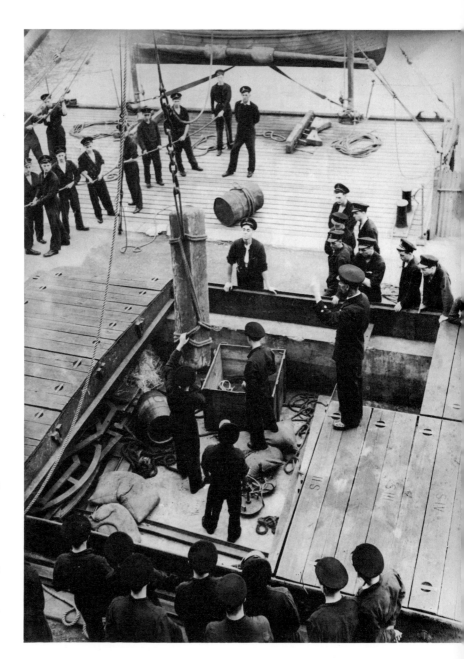

88. New Zealand soldiers on leave embark on the Thames for a sightseeing trip, June 1940. 'It will be a splendid episode in the history of the Empire if Australian, New Zealand and Canadian troops defend the Motherland against invasion', wrote Churchill.

89. The Merchant Navy, at risk from U-boats, aircraft and mines, was in the front line of battle. The photograph shows merchant seamen recruits being trained by the Royal Navy at 'HMS Gordon' – a rambling collection of buildings on dry land, with a pier.

90. Turning out small arms –
machine guns, rifles and revolvers
– at a Royal Ordnance factory,
November 1939.

91. Royal Ordnance factory: the
'big guns shop'.

92. Shell factory, November 1939.

93. WAAFS on duty at a Bomber Command Headquarters. The Women's Auxiliary Air Force, to give it its full name, was founded 28 June 1939 as a volunteer force and given military status in 1941. The women acted as balloon operators, airplane mechanics, radio-operators, parachute packers and did many other jobs short of actual combat. They numbered 182,000 at their peak in June 1943.

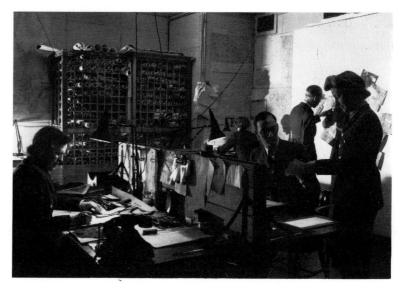

94. Packing parcels for sending to British prisoners of war. By the end of the war, roughly 200,000 prisoners from Britain and the Empire were held by the Germans and a further 108,000 by the Japanese. The arrival of the Red Cross parcel was a most important event in a prisoner's life.

95. Anti-aircraft gun control room, underground in London. As the ATS girls plotted the course of the aircraft, the army officer in charge issued orders to the gun sites to retaliate. The ATS (Auxiliary Territorial Service) were a corps of women volunteers formed in 1939; their chief work was at anti-aircraft sites. This photograph was issued to publicise 'Roof over Britain' – the official story of Britain's air defences 1939–42.

96. Women had joined the Navy for the first time in 1914, but the corps was disbanded after the First World War and not reactivated until 1939. Members of the Women's Royal Navy Service, affectionately known as Wrens, served throughout the war both on ship and on shore doing a variety of vital jobs, operating water ambulances, motor boats, ship-to-shore ferries, fleet mail boats; acting as cooks, mechanics, radio operators or administrators. These recruits were undergoing training on the east coast of England, May 1940.

97. Women also served on the land, growing food for Britain and enabling farm workers to join the armed forces. Land girls at work on a farm, carrying hay to feed the stock, during the hard winter days of early 1940.

98. At Wye College these girls were learning how to hitch implements to a tractor without losing a finger in the process.

99. A land girl driving a tractor during training at Wye College, a photograph to be much used in recruitment for the land army.

100. Twenty-three-year-old Mrs Robin Williamson, formerly engaged in poultry farming and dog-breeding, training in a government training centre to be a skilled aircraft fitter.

101. Nineteen-year-old shop assistants leaving London under a Ministry of Labour scheme to work in a munitions factory in the north of England, January 1942.

102. Sixteen-year-old member of the Home Guard, despatch rider Peter Derrick Willeringhaus, was 'mentioned in despatches for gallantry during enemy action' in January 1941, the first member of the Home Guard to achieve this distinction. Peter was delivering messages on his motor bike during a night air raid on London when a bomb blew him into the air. Although wounded and buried in debris he managed to free himself and run threequarters of a mile to deliver his message to headquarters before he collapsed.

103. The RAF taking delivery of an American Tomahawk I aircraft, 11 February 1941. Harry Hopkins, Roosevelt's envoy, had recently written to the President from England: 'People here are amazing from Churchill down, and if courage alone can win – the result will be inevitable. But they need our help desperately ...' Roosevelt had to act slowly, carrying American public opinion with him, but American aid was being steadily stepped up from 1939 until the end of 1941, when the Japanese attack on Pearl Harbor brought America into the war.

104. The British Expeditionary Force started to build up in France in September 1939; by the time the Germans attacked in May 1940 there were ten British divisions in the battle, five regular and five Territorial divisions – some 250,000 men. The white marks on the photograph are the censor's brush marks.

105. Churchill visiting a gun site on the north-eastern coast of England, 1942. Although the invasion never materialized, the threat of it remained and so did the defenders, often members of the Home Guard, until the war ended.

106. Pilots of Eagle Squadron, March 1941, in front of one of their Hurricane aircraft. This was an RAF Squadron composed of American pilots. Some of the American pilots had already flown against the Luftwaffe with the French airforce; others had been civilian airline pilots in the United States. This was the first Eagle Squadron; by October 1941 there were three, which continued to serve with the RAF until September 1942 when they were transferred to the US Air Force, taking their Spitfires with them.

107. The borough of Lewisham, in south-east London, raising money for the war effort.

108. One man and his dog. Anti-aircraft gunner John Gordon on leave with his dog 'Rob' who always remained with his master at his post, regardless of the roar of the AA batteries.

109. A Women's Voluntary Services group at work knitting blankets. The WVS, formed in May 1938, played a major role throughout the war feeding and clothing victims and workers in the Blitz, evacuating the homeless, operating mobile canteens and, as here, playing their part in 'make-do-and-mend' campaigns. 'The women in green were at least as important as, and probably considerably more in evidence than the Home Guard' (Professor Arthur Marwick).

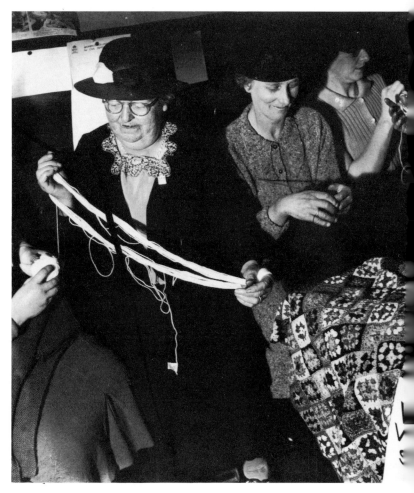

110. The first WAAFS, one a former veterinary nurse and the other a photographer, to go on duty as RAF policewomen, London, December 1941. When on plain-clothes duty they received a 'special allowance' of 3/6 (about 17p) a week.

111. ATS girls being trained to
drive heavy army lorries in the
north of England, January 1941.
After a three-week course, the
girls were entrusted with driving
the lorries in convoy to their units
throughout Britain.

112. Salvage: collection of shrapnel under the eye of a policeman.

113. Sidcup's salvage corps. Housewives were encouraged to keep several containers for their rubbish: one for metal, one for papers and cardboard, one for bones, one for edible waste to go to the pigs.

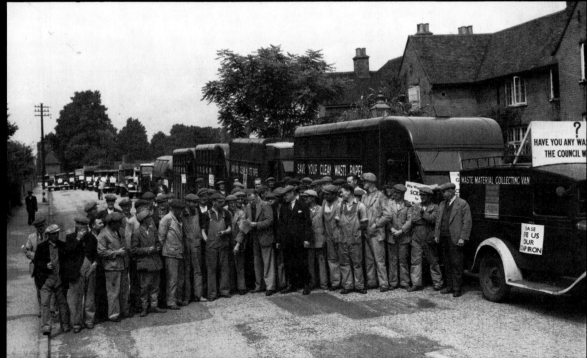

114. Even dodgem cars and ghost trains were taken to provide scrap metal and rubber for the war effort. This pile of dodgem cars came from a fairground at Skegness in Lincolnshire, April 1942.

115. Sidcup WVS collecting saucepans.

SEND YOUR PANS FLYING

5,000 *Make a* FIGHTER
25,000 .. .. BOMBER

116. Mystery bone for the 'Glue
for Aircraft' campaign. 'It must
have come from an elephant',
commented the salvage-collector,
Mr Aimes.

117. A mobile operating theatre, one of the few in existence at the time, August 1940 – on show at Erith.

118. King George VI at an anti-aircraft gun site during the Battle of Britain, one of his innumerable visits to military, naval and air force units all over the country throughout the war years.

119. Children could and did play their part in the war effort. In 1942, 600 girls and boys from London schools helped to bring in the harvest on 21 farms owned by the London County Council. The photograph shows Lord Latham, leader of the LCC with some of the children on the Chelsham Court Farm.

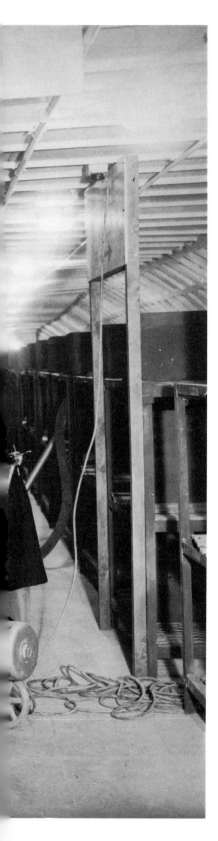

120. Cleaning a recently completed air-raid shelter for 800 people, a hundred feet beneath the streets of London, September 1942.

121. A cigarette for Sergeant Rich (sitting) from Pennsylvania after he received the Order of the Purple Heart from Major General Carl Spaatz. This was a US decoration for personnel killed or wounded by enemy action. Standing is 1st Lieut. Eugene M. Lockhart from South Carolina. Both were wounded in a daylight attack on shipyards in France. September 1942.

122. American troops parading through London in September 1942, the first time since 1917. Over 300 men were cheered all the way from Grosvenor Square to the Guildhall, where they were entertained to lunch by the Lord Mayor.

123. American Red Cross girls checking crockery before the opening of the Rainbow Club for American forces stationed in London, November 1942.

124. A cinema foyer was the site of this collection box for cigarettes for the troops overseas.

125. Mail bags for the troops being
loaded on to a BOAC flying boat
at Poole.

126. The all-American Eagle Squadrons, which originally served with the RAF, were transferred to the US Air Force in September 1942. Major Daymond, DFC and Bar, is shown wearing his old RAF 'Wings' and his new US badge after the transfer.

127. Air Chief Marshal Sir Sholto Douglas inspecting the Eagle Squadron pilots followed by the commander of the American Eighth Air Force, Carl Spaatz and by General Hunter.

128. Passers-by crowd around a Holborn shop displaying a map showing RAF attacks on Germany.

129. Naval cadets from HMS *Worcester* 1943, temporarily at Footscray Place, later destroyed by fire.

130. Over 1,500 Wrens paraded past the Queen outside Buckingham Palace as part of the service's fourth birthday celebrations. 11 April, 1943.

131. Part of the training for the invasion of Europe took place in Battersea bomb ruins, disguised as German streets, and complete with uniformed 'Nazis'.

132. American sailors and soldiers, on leave, walking through a London fog, Hyde Park, October 1943.

133. The American 'Flying Fortress' (Boeing B-17) spearheaded the daylight bombing offensive from 1943. 'Knock-Out Dropper', 13 November 1943.

134. General de Gaulle and the retired French Admiral, Emile Muselier, visiting the French destroyer *Le Triomphant*, one of the French ships in British ports in July 1940, following the fall of France. Most French sailors were so antagonized by the British attacks on the French Navy at Oran and Dakar that they refused to rally to de Gaulle, and the Free French navy never amounted to very much.

135. Some of the 3,000 American
sappers helping to demolish and
rebuild London's bombed houses
were visited by Duncan Sandys,
then Minister of Works, December
1944.

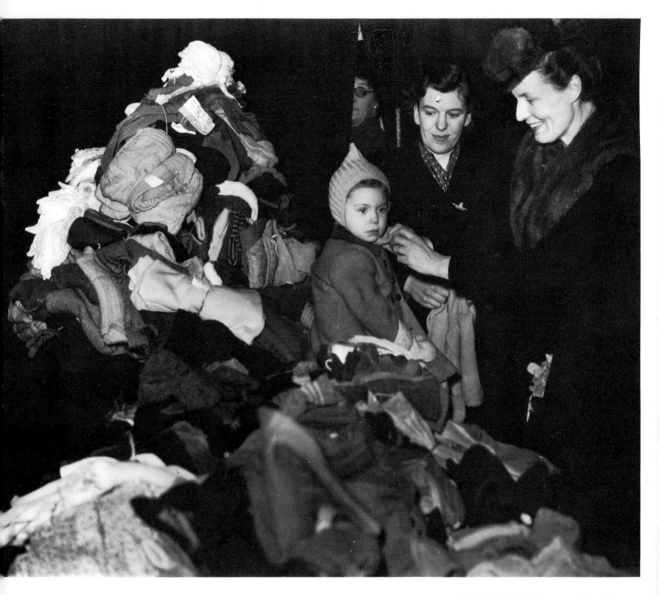

136. Dr Edith Summerskill, the Labour MP for West Fulham, giving out woollen clothes to 3,000 children under five. These clothes were the gift of women of Victoria, Australia. January 1945.

137. Cheeses arriving from America. Some of the cargo was a gift from the American people, some was lease-lend and some was from Canada.

138. The Queen with four-year-old Georgina Goddard wearing a cotton frock of a type being exported to the United States from Britain to gain dollars for the war effort. February 1941.

139. Christmas 1944: a welcome consignment of 300,000 toys and 25,000 boxes of sweets arrived from the British War Relief Society of America. The consignment was three times as large as in previous years in response to the terrible havoc wrecked by the flying bombs and the extra toys were allocated to the children of 'flying bomb alley'.

140. In the queue for the Australian gifts of woollen clothes a soldier can be seen with his small daughter. He was Sergeant Herbert Oakley, from Michigan, who had crossed into Canada in order to enlist on the outbreak of war. January 1945.

141. 'Canadian Corner', Orpington cemetery.

142. French and English in February 1945: from right to left, Georges Bidault, General de Gaulle's Foreign Minister, Rene Massigli, French Ambassador to Britain, Anthony Eden and Duff Cooper met to discuss the Yalta conference between America, Russia and Britain.

143. US airmen at their base in Britain, following a daylight bombing raid on Bretzdorf in Germany, March 1945. Colonel Milton, on the right, had been the first American airman to bomb Berlin. On the left is Major A.E. Strickland of Texas.

144. Royal mechanic. Princess
Elizabeth joined the ATS and in
April 1945 was learning car
maintenance watched by her
parents and her sister, Princess
Margaret.

5. Life Goes On

EVEN in the centre of the town there are aspects of rural life. While the buses roar along Oxford Street the gentler sounds of hens and ducks can be heard among the ruins of nearby Berners Street. There are pigs sleeping peacefully in improvised styes in the craters where seeds that have been buried for three hundred years have propagated themselves and make a display of purple milk-wort and willow-herb. The vicar of St James's, Piccadilly, counted twenty-three different varieties of wild plant behind his bombed altar.

Each evening at nine, everyone stops – as for the muezzin call to prayer in Mohammedan countries – for the evening news. It is almost an offence to telephone at the hour of the BBC bulletins, and as you walk along the pavements the announcer's voice echoes through all open windows. Every language is spoken on the pavements, and in some parts the English voice is seldom heard. Baseball crowds cheer in Hyde Park while in the long twilight of double summer-time Piccadilly Circus is transformed by the khaki figures squatting along the wall of sandbags around Eros's statue, into the sleepy Southland from which many of these raw recruits have come.

CECIL BEATON, *Diaries*, September 1944.

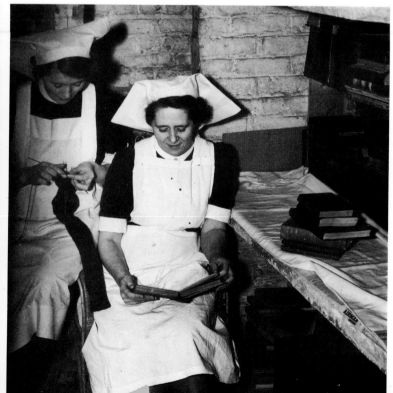

145. Nurses at Richmond Hospital, 1940, whiling away time in the hospital shelter with books and knitting.

146. Wendell Wilkie with a tin-hatted policeman on his fact-finding visit of February 1941. The AA had put up a sign 'To The Trenches' pointing towards a London park. The AA also put up helpful road signs for our troops in France.

147. During the Blitz, Oxford
provided a haven for many
evacuees, queuing here outside a
Lyons tea room.

148. Cricket at Eltham was unaffected by the presence of a barrage balloon on the ground, 1940.

149. The Women's League of Health and Beauty exercising in gas masks.

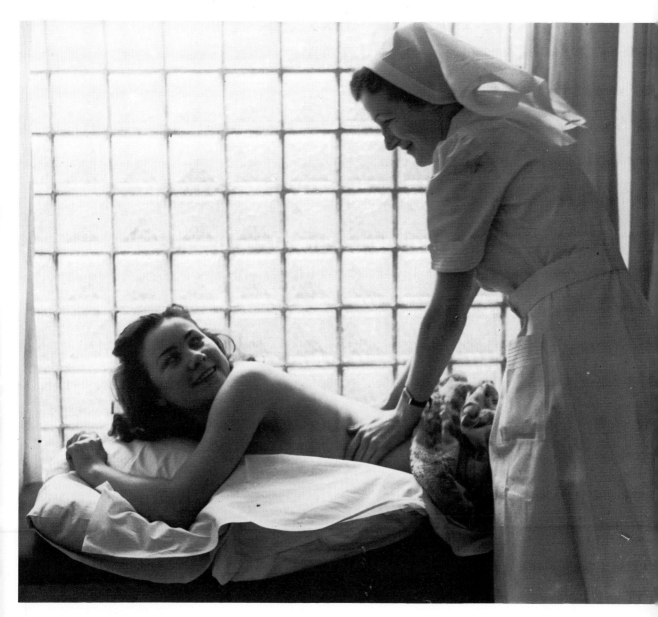

150. In the dark days of December
1940, the spirits of ARP workers
in Finsbury were improved by
violet ray sunlamps, massage and
hot showers.

152. Christmas dinner, 1939, with no shortage of whisky. The government was reluctant to introduce rationing prematurely in order that morale be sustained at as high a level as possible.

153. Wounded French soldiers in an English hospital, 23 June 1940, receiving their ration of red wine, carefully measured out by the nurse.

151. In a sergeant's mess at a depot in Kent, November 1939.

155. A schoolboy, smiling through, sweeping up outside his bombed home at Northfleet.

154. Wounded sailor, date unknown.

156. A smile for the cameras from a
London Transport worker and his
family, Bromley, Kent.

157. Even in December 1940
Charlton was able to play Arsenal.
Originally there was a ban on
football during periods of 'Alert'
but this proved too much for the
fans. Play was therefore allowed
to continue under the watchful
eye of a trained 'spotter' who
would give warning of an
imminent air-raid.

158. Gunners with an anti-aircraft coastal battery were rehearsing the can-can for a charity Christmas show in early 1941 when the alarm went. The dancers, some managing to collect a steel helmet, had to run to man the guns. This picture was censored.

159. These can-can dancers were
young men from the RAF
rehearsing for a revue at the Arts
Theatre, Cambridge in December
1940. The producer (right) was
Freddie Carpenter, and the
proceeds went to the Air Force
Fund.

160. The WAAFs (Women's
Auxiliary Air Force) put on a
pantomime for Christmas 1940
with guest star Wing Commander
Evan Evans (right) as Cinderella
and Aircrafts-woman Green as
Robin Hood. This picture was also
censored.

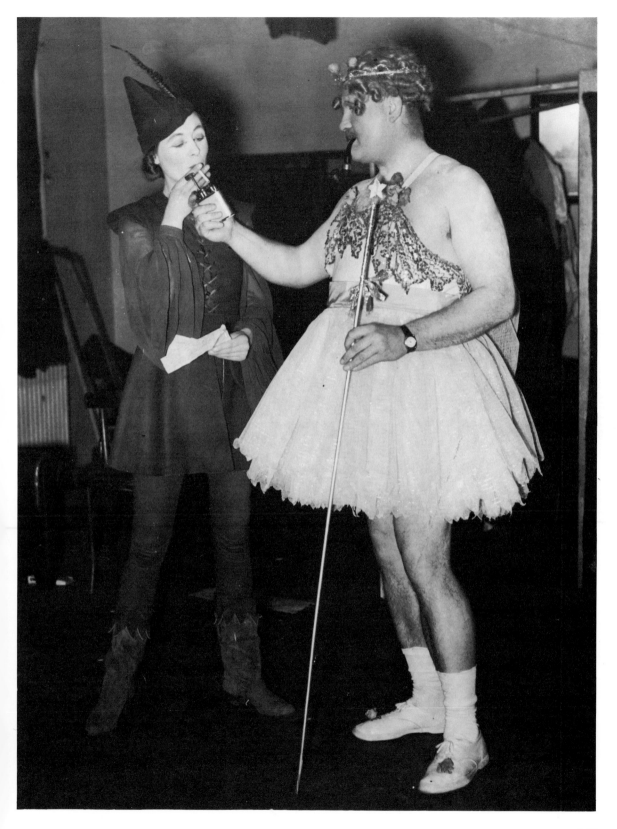

163. Toyshop, Christmas 1940, displaying models of servicemen, guns, aircraft and barrage balloons.

161. The company of London's only professional pantomine for the Christmas of 1940, 'Aladdin'.

162. Looking forward to the future: schoolboys with their model of a utopian town incorporating wide tracts of open countryside, trees, farms, hedgerows, winding lanes and a single track railway. The plans won them first prize in a Council competition.

164. A farmer on horseback riding
through floods of March 1940.

165. The crowds in London's
Petticoat Lane Sunday market
which was in full swing,
December 1940.

166. Live geese being auctioned in
Bethnal Green, Christmas 1940.

167. The Christmas mail at Mount
Pleasant, 1940. In the background
can be seen the soldiers who had
come to help the post-office girls
sorting the mountain of parcels.

168. Fifteen-year-old milk girl
Rose Brown of Walworth, 1941.
She had taken the place of the
milkman who had been called up.

169. Bombed-out dogs and other pets were cared for by the RSPCA, February 1941.

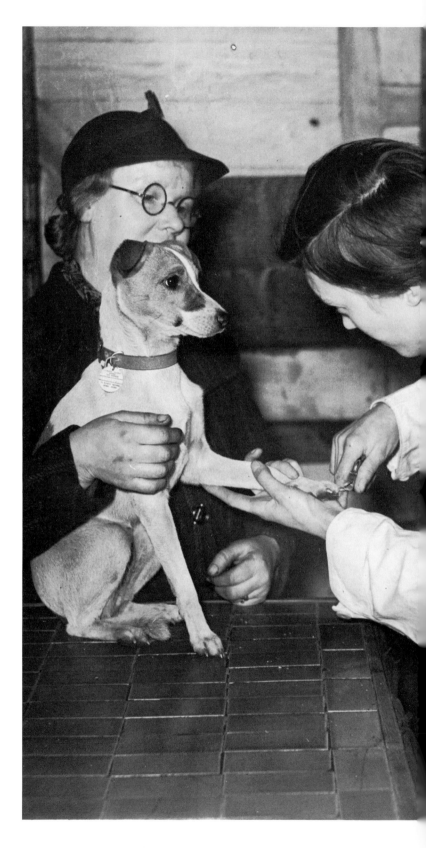

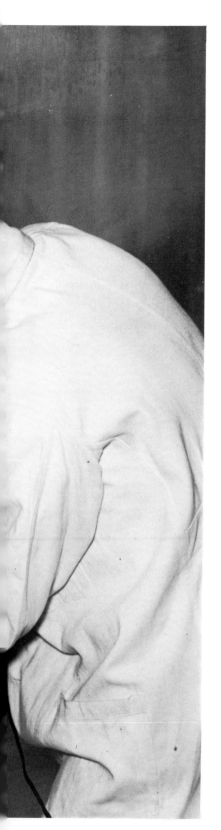

170. Postwomen adjusting their hats; their uniform was blue serge with scarlet piping. February 1941.

171. Soldiers singing at a party for
the troops.

172. Soldiers singing at home in
Erith.

173. One of the lighter moments
for the Deptford Auxiliary Fire
Service: the grand finale chorus
of their Concert Party.

174. French girls of the Corps Femina, the Free French counterpart of the ATS, at their headquarters in London.

175. An American who could not wait for the United States to declare war, Corporal Lowell Bennett of New Jersey, at his wedding to an English girl, February 1941. Corporal Lowell Bennett drove an American ambulance during the Battle of France, was awarded the Croix de Guerre for gallantry and was taken prisoner. On his release he came to England to join the Free French army and met his future bride, a helper at the American Eagle Club in London.

176. Sailor marries soldier.

177. In February 1941 Lord
Inchcape married Pixie Hannay,
the widow of Pilot Officer Patrick
Hannay who was killed during
the Battle of Britain the previous
year.

178. Football match between Dutch and Belgian servicemen in Britain at Walthamstow, which took place in the presence of Prince Bernhard of the Netherlands, 1941.

179. Bernard Carter of the American Red Cross acted as Santa Claus to bombed-out children, Christmas 1941.

180. Girls of the Windmill Theatre
preparing for a show. The
Windmill's boast was 'we never
closed' and it provided shows
throughout the war.

181. A Windmill girl on stage
during a show for the troops.

182. A Morrison shelter being used as a ping-pong table. These shelters were developed in 1941 for use by those who had no garden in which to erect the very effective Anderson shelters. At a pinch they could hold four adults and could be made tolerably comfortable with a mattress and flaps that came down the sides to protect against flying glass and debris.

183. Augustus John in London, autumn 1941. He was an official war artist in the First World War but was judged too uncooperative to be commissioned during the Second World War.

184. The messenger boys of Cable
and Wireless formed a brass band,
shown here playing outside a
hospital to entertain the patients,
December 1941.

185. The Mayor and Mayoress of
Dartford entertained 400 poor
children to tea at the Co-operative
Hall, December 1940. Santa Claus
welcomed the children, the Mayor
and Mayoress poured out tea and
jellies proved as popular as ever.

186. To mark the American entry into the war, underwear embroidered with the American flag went on sale, 1942.

187. Commemorating the second anniversary of the Battle of Britain in the ruins of a blitzed church in Stepney, September 1942.

188. ENSA (Entertainment National Service Association) was formed at the beginning of the war to provide professional entertainers for the forces and war workers. It was ENSA that staged a dramatic entertainment on the steps of St Paul's Cathedral to brighten the dull days of 1942. Music was provided by massed choirs and military bands, conducted by Sir Henry Wood, and many celebrated actors and actresses took part.

189. Little Ray Styles wearing the
DSM which had just been
awarded to his father, Petty
Officer R. G. Styles.

190. Sir Alexander Korda,
recently arrived from America in
a bomber, met his wife, the film
actress Merle Oberon, in London,
September 1942. They were
together only for a few hours, as
Merle Oberon was on tour of the
camps of England and Northern
Ireland, entertaining the troops.

191. Deborah Kerr, red-haired
leading lady of the British cinema,
kept hens and dug her garden to
supplement wartime rations. Her
wartime films included: *Major
Barbara*; *Love on the Dole*; *Hatter's
Castle* and *The Life and Death of
Colonel Blimp*. After the war
Deborah Kerr went to Hollywood
where she had a long and highly
successful career.

192. Vera Lynn at home, 1942.

193. John Mills, his wife and daughter in the garden of their house in Kent. At this time he was an extremely popular actor, with leading roles in *Goodbye Mr Chips* (1939); *In Which We Serve* (1942); *This Happy Breed* (1944) and *The Way to the Stars* (1945).

194. Margot Fonteyn at the age of 21 was already the supreme British ballerina, having made her debut with the Vic-Wells ballet in 1934 when only fifteen.

195. Schools continued to function, but each child had a gas mask on his desk and no more children could be taught than there were shelters for.

196. Corporal McCall of Stirling, wounded at El Alamein, with his wife after receiving the Military Medal at Buckingham Palace. This was the turning point of the war in Africa. 'Up to Alamein we survived. After Alamein we conquered,' wrote Winston Churchill.

197. The 1943 petrol shortage did
not stop these enterprising race-
goers from reaching Windsor for
the opening of the flat racing
season; they travelled by boat.

198. The premiere of *Fanny By
Gaslight* was celebrated by a party
given at Claridges by Mr James
Rank, May 1944.

199. New Zealand VAD
(Voluntary Aid Detachment)
nurses, all serving on a hospital
ship, talking to the Duchess of
Kent, October 1944.

200. The WVS providing household goods for bombed-out families in London from gifts sent by provincial towns, 1945.

201. An 'all-electric kitchen' designed by the British Electrical Development Association was on show in January 1945. Kettle, clock, stove and washing machine were electric; the mangle, however, was hand-powered.

202. British restaurants were open
all over London to provide good
food at minimum prices. Here, at
the Bethnal Green Museum, 1,000
hot lunches were served every
day; the price was a shilling a
time.

203. By March 1945 the thoughts of women in the Services were turning to the 180 clothing coupons each would receive on demobilization. An enterprising store laid on a fashion show to help them with their choice.

204. One item in the show was the 'utility' fur coat at £24. 'Utility' clothes and furniture were made to certain specifications which saved on raw materials; for instance, men's trousers were made without turn-ups.

6. The End in Sight

HOSTILITIES will end officially at one minute after midnight tonight (Tuesday), but in the interest of saving lives the 'Cease Fire' began yesterday to be sounded all along the front, and our dear Channel Islands are also to be freed today. . . . Today, perhaps, we shall think mostly of ourselves. Tomorrow we shall pay a particular tribute to our Russian comrades whose prowess in the field has been one of the grand contributions to the general victory. The German war is therefore at an end. After years of preparation, Germany hurled herself upon Poland . . . and in pursuance of our guarantee to Poland, and in agreement with the French Republic, Great Britain, the British Empire and Commonwealth of Nations, declared war upon this foul aggression. After gallant France had been struck down, we, from this island and our united Empire, maintained the struggle single-handed for a whole year until we were joined by the military might of Soviet Russia and later by the overwhelming power and resources of the United States of America. Finally, almost the whole world was combined against the evil-doers who are now prostrate before us. Our gratitude to our splendid allies goes forth from all our hearts in this island and throughout the British Empire. We may allow ourselves a brief period of rejoicing, but let us not forget for a moment the toil and efforts that lie ahead. Japan, with all her treachery and greed, remains unsubdued. The injury she has inflicted on Great Britain, the United States, and other countries, and her detestable cruelties call for justice and retribution. We must now devote all our strength and resources to the completion of our task, both at home and abroad. Advance, Britannia! Long live the cause of freedom! God save the King!

WINSTON CHURCHILL'S victory in Europe broadcast   8 May 1945

205. Part of the vast paraphernalia accumulated in the south of England as British, Canadian and American troops prepared for 'Overlord', the invasion of Normandy, history's greatest amphibious operation, which took place on 'D' Day, 6 June 1944.

206. British troops training for the invasion, 'somewhere in England'.

207. American troops embarking
for Normandy.

208. As the Allies fought their way
across Europe, reinforcements
arrived from the United States
and after a few days left British
ports for the western front.

209. December 1944: British soldiers, home on leave from Italy, arrive at St Pancras Station.

210. January 1945: the first contingent of men on leave from the western front arrived in England to receive this welcome.

211. The homecoming of Private Bill Martin from Burma, where he had been serving in the Royal Army Medical Corps. The flags had been flying at his home in Kilburn for a month, ever since his mother (left, in a print apron) had received the news of his imminent return. His four sisters had spent many long hours at Euston Station, waiting for leave trains and hoping to see their brother – the joy that shines from their faces speaks more clearly than any words.

212. German prisoners of war were a common sight in Britain as the war neared its end. This group was clearing snow from the roads in January 1945.

213. Captain Oscar O'Neill of the US Airforce, recently freed from Stalag Luft 3, married an English actress, Irene Taylor, on 19 May 1945.

I SMELL PINEAPPLE

Daily Mail

VICTORY EDITION

TUESday FIELD-DAY

NO. 15,290 ONE PENNY FOR KING AND EMPIRE TUESDAY, MAY 8, 1945

3-POWER ANNOUNCEMENT TO-DAY; BUT BRITAIN KNEW LAST NIGHT

VE-DAY—IT'S ALL OVER

All quiet till 9 p.m.—then the London crowds went mad in the West End

THE Face of Victory—by day and night: Roadways in and around Piccadilly-circus were jammed nearly solid yesterday afternoon by crowds waiting to hear VE-Day announced. Then they decided not to wait—they began to celebrate. These Daily Mail pictures give you a vivid impression of the great concourse of joy—above by day; on the left, by night. Other scenes—Pages THREE and FOUR.

PM put off the big speech UNTIL TO-DAY

By WILSON BROADBENT, Diplomatic Correspondent

GERMANY surrendered unconditionally to the Allies yesterday. But there will be no official announcement of victory until 3 p.m. to-day—officially described as VE-Day—when Mr. Churchill will give the news to the world.

He will follow this with an address to the House of Commons, and at 9 p.m. the King will speak to Britain and the Empire.

Mr. Churchill's private room at the House of Commons was last night "wired-up" so that if he wishes he can make his broadcast from there.

To-day's announcement will be made simultaneously in London, Washington, and Moscow. To-day, therefore, is the first of the promised two-days V-holiday for the country.

Broadcasts will also be made by General Eisenhower and Field-Marshals Montgomery and Alexander.

Mr. Churchill's two statements to-day will not affect his intention to broadcast at length on Thursday night, the 5th anniversary of his assumption of the Premiership.

After his statement in the House of Commons, Mr Churchill will propose the adjournment of business while M.P.s attend a special Service of Thanksgiving at St. Margaret's Church, Westminster. They will then return to the House of Commons, adjourn, and arrange to meet again on Wednesday.

Until shortly before 6 o'clock last night it was fully expected that Mr. Churchill would be able to announce the news that the war was over.

Victory lunch

He had been standing by the microphone from some time after 3 o'clock, and everything was ready for him to break [illegible] the normal programmes of the B.B.C.

Earlier in the day he had been speaking on the Transatlantic telephone to Washington, and he also had several calls to Moscow. His object was to obtain an agreed time for releasing the big news.

There had been a previous agreement that there should be simultaneous times for release. Apparently in London it was understood that Monday would be suitable to all concerned.

In anticipation of this important occasion Mr Churchill gave a special Victory luncheon party at No. 10 Downing-street for the Chiefs of Staff whose health he personally proposed.

After luncheon Mr. Churchill was ready to broadcast, but no news of Washington's or Moscow's assent had been received.

It was nearly 6 o'clock when it was learned that both the United States and the Soviet Government were in favour of postponing the formal announcing until this afternoon.

Moscow preferred this course because of certain final formalities connected with the German surrender, which will take place to-day. Washington had other reasons which are not yet known. So Mr. Churchill, finding himself in a minority, had to agree.

CZECHS TOLD TO 'SMASH GERMANS'

Czech-controlled radio early to-day appealed to Patriots at the barricades to attack and smash German positions. Radio declared that "Protector" Frank yesterday made "arrogant" offer to resign and ordered that [illegible] barricades.—Reuter.

TARAKAN NEARLY CUT IN TWO

Manila, Tuesday.—Allies cleared ground east of the main oilfield on Tarakan, off Borneo, and advanced across the island to within a mile and a half of the east shore. Fighting continues for Tarakan town.—B.U.P.

U.S. made it VE-Day all the same

Work walk-out

From DON IDDON, Daily Mail Correspondent

New York, Monday.

THIS was VE-Day in the U.S.—official or not.

The celebrations began in New York at breakfast-time, a few minutes after word came from Rheims, France, that Germany had surrendered unconditionally to Britain, the United States, and Russia.

They went on all day despite an avalanche of confused messages, lack of official confirmation, half-denials, and a barrage of rumours that the surrender was a hoax.

The American public, and particularly the New York public, this time was determined that this was the end of the war in Europe, and resolved to commemorate it.

The first reaction, and it was the same all over Manhattan, was to fab open windows, tear up telephone directories, and hurl paper into the streets.

For hours tons upon tons of ticker tape, torn-up newspapers, envelopes, letters, magazines, and in some instances hats and waste-paper baskets, cascaded down.

Jammed roads

Tens of thousands of people abandoned work and rushed into the Times-square area, shouting and singing. Motorists blew their hooters, factory whistles shrieked, and in New York Bay ships sounded their sirens.

Bands of Service men and girls paraded the avenues, waving flags, shouting and yelling, planting kisses on strangers, cavorting in and out of bars.

Great stores, offices, the banks, the factories closed down as staffs walked out en masse.

Traffic was completely tied up in mid-town as throngs of gesticulating, laughing people jammed roadways, jumped on to the running-boards of private cars, taxis, and buses.

At first city officials, led by Mayor La Guardia, attempted to curb the jubilation.

Over the radio came a reminder that there was nothing official, that it was merely a report which had declared that war in Europe was over. The people ignored the advice.

Daily Mail

IN accordance with the expressed wishes of the Government that workers generally should enjoy a day's holiday following the announcement of the cessation of hostilities in Europe, The Daily Mail, in common with other London morning newspapers, will not be published [illegible]

SYMBOL of the mood of London, this man, at the top of a lamp-post, waves a flag above the crowds.—Daily Mail picture.

The war still goes on here—

PRAGUE BOMBED AS SS SHOOT CZECH CIVILIANS

GERMAN bombs are falling on Prague for the first time as the war in Europe enters its last hours. In defiance of surrender orders, German forces in Czecho-Slovakia are fighting on. They are venting their last spite on the Czechs, shooting them down ruthlessly in the streets of the capital.

Refugees from Prague who have reached Allied-occupied Pilsen say that, in many cases, the S.S. went through the city driving people out of their houses into the streets.

And there other S.S. men mowed them down with machine-guns. The S.S., according to the refugees, know they will probably be executed when caught and have abandoned all normal conduct.

That the S.S. are completely out of hand is indicated in a broadcast by the German commander in Bohemia and Moravia warning his troops to respect international law.

Two columns of General Patton's tanks are racing to Prague's rescue and were last reported seven miles [illegible] of the capital.

A Czech Spitfire squadron and formations of large aircraft carrying Czech ground troops have left Britain for Czecho-Slovakia.

Broadcasting from London last night, Dr. Hubert Ripka, Czecho-Slovak Minister of Foreign Trade, said that, by fighting on after the general capitulation, the Germans had placed themselves beyond the law and would be dealt with as saboteurs.

Pilsen kisses

PILSEN, Monday.

LIEUT.-GENERAL MAJEWLSKI, commanding the German garrison [illegible]

BACK PAGE—Col. EIGHT →

Beacon chain begun by Piccadilly's bonfires

By GUY RAMSEY

LONDON, dead from six until nine, suddenly broke into victory life last night. Suddenly, spontaneously, deliriously. The people of London, denied VE-Day officially, held their own jubilation. "VE-Day may be to-morrow," they said, "but the war is over to-night." Bonfires blazed from Piccadilly to Wapping.

The sky once lit by the glare of the blitz shone red with the Victory glow. The last trains departed from the West End unregarded. The pent-up spirits of the throng, the polyglot throng that is London in war-time, burst out, and by 11 o'clock the capital was ablaze with enthusiasm.

Processions formed up out of nowhere, disintegrating for no reason, to re-form somewhere else. Waving flags, marching in step, with linked arms or half-embraced, the people strode down the great thoroughfares—Piccadilly, Regent-street, the Mall, to the portals of Buckingham Palace.

They marched and counter-marched so as not to get too far from the centre. And from them, in harmony and discord, rose song. The songs of the last war, the songs of a century ago. The songs of the beginning of this war—"Roll out the Barrel" and "Tipperary"; "Ilkla Moor" and "Loch Lomond"; "Bless 'em All" and "Pack Up Your Troubles."

ROCKETS AND SONGS

Rockets—found no-one knows where, set-off by no-one knows whom—streaked into the sky, exploding not in death but a burst of scarlet fire. A pile of straw filled with thunder-flashes salvaged from some military dump spurted and exploded near Leicester-square.

Every car that challenged the milling, moiling throng was submerged in humanity. They climbed on the running-boards, on the bonnet, on the roof. They hammered on the panels. They shouted and sang.

Against the drumming on metal came the clash of cymbals, improvised out of dustbin lids. The dustbin itself was a football for an impromptu Rugger scrum. Bubbling, exploding with gaiety, the people "mafficked." Headlights silhouetted couples kissing, couples cheering, couples waving flags.

Every cornice, every lamp-post was scaled. Americans marched with A.T.S. girls in civvies, fresh from their work benches, ran by the side of battle-dressed

Continued in Back Page, Col. 6

SCHACHT SAVED BY 'FIFTH'

Niemoller, too

Daily Mail Special Correspondent

ALLIED H.Q., Italy, Monday.

SOME of the most famous victims of Nazi-ism have been rescued by the Fifth Army from the Prager Wildsee prison camp, near Obbiaco, Italy.

Among them was **Pastor Niemoller**, head of the German Confessional Church, whose defiance of Hitler led to a seven years' incarceration in concentration camps.

A few hours after his release Pastor Niemoller held a service in the lounge of a hotel.

His text was the words of Isaiah:

For the mountains shall depart, and the hills be removed; but my kindness shall not depart from thee, neither shall the covenant of my peace be removed, saith the Lord that hath mercy on thee.

In all, the Fifth Army saved 120 hostages, including **Dr. Schuschnigg**, former Chancellor of Austria who during the week-end was erroneously reported to have been executed.

Dr. Schuschnigg's wife was also found. **M. Léon Blum**, former Socialist Premier of France, and his wife, were also freed.

'Evil Hitler'

The camp in which these famous people were found was a smallish affair—a group of huts around a chateau on a hillside. But behind its barbed wire the Fifth Army men found many high officers—Greek, Russian, Hungarian—and a number of Germans including **Dr. Schacht**, former German Minister of Finance and President of the Reichsbank.

Asked if Hitler was sane, Dr. Schacht said: "In some things no, in others he is a genius."

Someone suggested an evil genius, and Schacht said: "Yes, an evil genius . . . an evil and diabolical genius."

VE-WEATHER

Strait of Dover yesterday: Victory weather, with hours of sunshine. Day temperature, 60deg.

GOEBBELS' BODY IN A SHELTER

GOEBBELS, the German Propaganda Minister, his wife, and five children have been found dead in Berlin.

Moscow says that their bodies were found in an air-raid shelter near the Reichstag, and it has been established that all died of poisoning.

No trace has been found of the bodies of Hitler or Göring.

There was speculation in London last night whether the Nazi leaders may have fled to a place of hiding.

It was pointed out, however, that their bodies may have been destroyed in the wreckage of the burning Chancellery or some other building.

Moscow radio last night reported, says B.U.P., that troops had penetrated deep into an underground fortress in the basement of Hitler's Chancellery.

"Smoke is pouring from an unexplored depth into which we had been unable to penetrate," said the radio.

MONTY MEETS ROKOSSOVSKY

4 toasts at lunch

TWENTY-FIRST ARMY GROUP, Monday.—Field-Marshal Montgomery lunched to-day with Marshal Konstantin Rokossovsky at Wismar.

Toasts were drunk to the Allied armies, Mr Churchill, Marshal Stalin, and President Truman.—Reuter.

Home by searchlight

There will be a searchlight display by the A.A. over Central London and London suburbs on VE-Night, from 11.45 p.m. to 12.15 a.m. and again on the next night at the same time.

ARRESTED POLES MAY BE TRIED BY LUBLIN

LUBLIN radio said yesterday that the Polish Provisional Government may demand that General Okulicki and others of the 16 Poles arrested by the Russians be tried both in Warsaw and Moscow for high treason.

The radio said: "Public opinion in Poland has received with indignation the news of the action of Okulicki and his accomplices, who are accused of carrying out diversionary activities against the Red Army.

"Because the criminal activities of Okulicki and his accomplices were also directed against the reborn Polish State, it constitutes high treason.

"The Provisional Government reserves the right to demand that Okulicki and his accomplices be turned over to the Polish authorities to be indicted in the courts of the Republic as well."

M. Mikolajczyk, former Polish Prime Minister in London, announced yesterday that he is preparing a statement on the arrests.

He said that the arrested men cannot be accused of diversionary acts against the Soviet forces, as they were sincere partisans of a Polish-Soviet understanding.

214. VE Day, 8 May 1945: the front page of the *Daily Mail* announced the jubilation of the previous night when both America and Britain had celebrated in advance of the official announcement.

215. Churchill arriving at the House of Commons for the addresses of congratulations to the King on the victory in Europe from the Commons and the Lords.

216. Whitehall on VE Day:
Churchill with the members of his
cabinet appearing on the balcony
of the Ministry of Health. The
crowds roared their approval
when Churchill appeared and sang
'For He's a Jolly Good Fellow'.

217. They had to make do with a portrait of Churchill in Charlton-on-Medlock in Lancashire.

218. Piccadilly Circus: a young American soldier hugging an old Englishwoman.

219. Churchill, the architect of
victory, cheered by the crowd on
VE Day in Whitehall.

220. May 16: Field Marshal
Montgomery, back in England,
cuts a victory cake at the Mansion
House when celebrating the
diamond jubilee of the Gordon
Boys' School, Woking, of which
he was president. Sir Frank
Alexander, the Lord Mayor and
the Lady Mayoress are with him.

221. Euston Station, 17 May 1945.
Lieutenant-General Scheurlein,
the former German commander in
Macedonia, wearing his grey army
cloak, was one of a number of
senior German Officers passing
through London.

222. Workers starting to remove
some of the 80,000 sandbags
which were protecting the
treasures of Westminster Abbey.
The Abbey survived the war
without serious harm, although
many of the surrounding
buildings – the Dean's house, the
Cloisters, the buildings of
Westminster School and the Choir
School – were destroyed or badly
damaged.

223. Thanksgiving service for victory in Europe in the shattered church of St Mary-le-Bow, Cheapside.

224. Churchill resigned as Prime
Minister on 23 May 1945 and
formed a caretaker Conservative
government. The election
campaign started at once;
Churchill here was in his
constituency, Woodford, in Essex,
acknowledging the cheers of the
crowd with his wife by his side.
At the election, however, the
Labour party swept into power
with a landslide victory.

225. The King and Queen, with
Princess Elizabeth, attended a
farewell parade of the Civil
Defence organizations in Hyde
Park. Thousands of men and
women, and even a contingent of
rescue dogs, came from all over
the country to join in the parade.
The King was photographed as he
inspected be-medalled policemen,
June 1945.

226. Belgian refugees on their way
home, many with children who
had never been in their native
land. The proud father with the
baby was Clement Young from
Mauritius, who had come to
England, joined the RAF,and met
and married his Belgian wife,
Raymonde.

227. Demobilization: the first men
to be 'demobbed' from the RAF
receiving their documents at
Uxbridge, Middlesex. 18 June
1945.

228. The men then left Uxbridge for the RAF Civilian Clothing Centre at Wembley, where they were measured for their civilian clothes.

229. Leaving the Civilian Clothing Centre, the RAF and the war behind, the men set off down Civvy Street.

230. The Royal Artillery in the suburbs, practising for the great victory parade.

231. 8 June 1946: the United States
contingent in the victory parade.

232. British Empire contingents in
the parade, swinging into the
Victoria Embankment from
Northumberland Avenue,
London.

233. Tanks entering the Mall, where the King took the salute. 21,000 Allied troops took part in the parade, with many famous commanders. There were also contingents from these who had fought on the Home Front.